THE LAST MAGICIAN

STEPHEN COREY

Revised Edition

Swallow's Tale Press

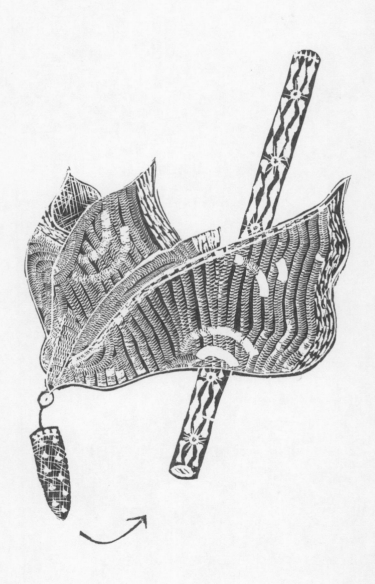

THe
LAST
MAGICIAN
STePHeN
COReY

art
Coco Gordon

foreword
Charles Fishman

ACKNOWLEDGMENTS

The author thanks the editors of the following periodicals in which some of the poems in this collection were first published. In some cases the poems appear in slightly different forms.

The American Poetry Review	"Praying Mantises"
The Ark	"Gifts"
	"Nude Man Tosses Meat from Truck"
California Quarterly	"The Taxidermy Shop"
College of Charleston Miscellany	"The Butcher's Daughter to Her Lover"
The Devil's Millhopper	"Teresa's Doll with Broken Arm and Comb"
The Florida Review	"The Last Magician"
	"Tooth"
	"The World's Largest Poet Visits Rural Idaho"
The Georgia Review	"Carpenter: Of His Pleasures"
	"Potter"
	"Quilts"
	"Smith"
	"State Craft Fair: Berea, Kentucky"
	"Whittler to His Lover"
Jamestown Post-Journal	"My Daughter's Night"
Kudzu	"Self-Destructing Poem"
Southern Poetry Review	"The Lovers Visit the Museum"
	"Migration"
	"Sitting on Each Other's Laps"
	"Tracking Deer with My Daughters"

The author thanks the following people for their editorial and personal support in bringing this book to completion: Paul Edward Allen, James Brooks, Richard Campbell, Brandon Kershner, Jr., Milton Kessler, Robert Kroetsch, Robert Steinem, Edward Wilson. And, Mary, Heather, and Miranda.

Art by Coco Gordon. Typeset in Garamond by Barbara Shaw and CLS Printing. Revised edition, with minor emendations introduced by the author. Printed in U.S.A. by CLS Printing, Tallahassee, FL.

Copies of this book may be had by sending $7.95 for paperback or $13.95 for hardbound, plus $1.00 postage, to:

> **Swallow's Tale Press**
> 736 Greenwillow Run
> Wesley Chapel, Florida 34249

Library of Congress Number: 87-60412
ISBN 0-930501-16-0 (cloth)
0-930501-17-9 (paper)

For Robert Dana and Lola Haskins

CONTENTS

FOREWORD

TOWARDS OTHER LIVES

Often, it seems that we hold a whip in hand when encountering the emerging presence of an artist. With this whip, we urge the young writer to appear, in his life and in his work, like an uncharted planet; we goad him to move toward an extravagance of style or content or voice that, with numbing predictability, palls to an irritating sameness. Too soon, we tire of his tamed originality. We light no candles for his longevity, wishing rather for a comet than for a true star of the spirit that might burn with a clear, steady brilliance. Often, it seems that we hold two whips: with the first, we encourage flights of unparalleled soaring, no matter the risks; with the second, we strive to keep the poet from transgressing the known limits, for we will not rest until both he and his work have been securely anchored to one mapped latitude or another.

Perhaps it is time to restate the obvious: a good new body of poetry seems important to us precisely because it excites what has once been awakened. The doors to vision swing open at the sounding of the secret note that is forever forgotten and rediscovered, the lost chord of perception; or they burst open before desire honed to an edge that is, in its austere simplicity, impossible to duplicate or will. Not new forms, eccentric spellings, reworkings of the myths; not baroque line breaks or broken rules. No rules. But a voice that articulates the mystery of being, whose intimate contrariness we know. Not new, but *near*: near the vulnerable and authentic.

Yet we require a certain amplitude, a presence: the poet should wake us from the sleep of the ordinary. We resist what Robert Peters has called "books of snivelling first persons." We wait for the writer who moves towards other lives. Stephen Corey is such a writer. He has the self-effacing power that permits an artist to forego the exotic and extraordinary for the savor of what can be known. Poem after poem, Corey leads us into a familiar landscape and helps us remember it, so that we can make it ours. This is the special gift *The Last Magician* brings to us.

—Charles Fishman

I CRAFTS

EMBROIDERY

Nothing less than painting by thread—
needling hawks to cover a cowboy's chest,
nightingales for a regal cloak,
daisies for the pillow of a child.

Like the best of lovers,
the threads interweave and overlay
but cannot be fused on any palette—
each bright line unique
as the music of broid.

SMITH

I go to church on the rims of carriage wheels,
into the chest on the scalpel.
I am hinged and latched to every village home,
hammered deep into my own hammer.

Call me farrier on a cloudy day
and I just might split your skull—
better call the poet a printer's devil.
If the sun is right I'll spare you, sit you down
while I forge a Swedish lock and key.

What non-living things re-create themselves?
Tools. Tools the others must have to begin.
What can I do that lovers only dream?
Fuse two things into one, forever.
Would you turn your back on me?
Go then. But remember: the world is mounted
on the rainbow of firing iron—from black
to palest yellow, through blues and reds to blazing white—
and only I can read the shade
between bend and break, shape and ruin.

QUILTS

One woman wept, they say,
when a peddler reached her cabin
with no new patterns to sell.

Irish Chain, Persian Pear, Rose of Tennessee

I still make my bed with *Kansas Troubles* —
I was only five when Mother said
"Twelve you must have in your hope chest, before
the Bridal Quilt, and that before you'll wed."
First my stitches tried to mirror hers,
our hands touching as we worked.
At night she plucked mine out
to keep her project whole.
Next came simple sewings: double lines
and scallops on my own crazy quilt.

Bear Track, Turkey Track, Beauty of Kaintuck

Some days, when Tommy and Jimmy ran outside
shouting off the chickens, I thought
I'd stretched myself across that frame, waiting
for the womenfolk to pad and quilt and bind me.
Yet with all the years of work,
when the time came Joseph had to wait
seven months while I finished *Jacob's Tears.*
The Bridal must be perfect, Mother warned.
A broken thread, a crop gone bad;
a twisted stitch, a baby dead.

Wreath of Grapes, Flying Swallows, Pomegranate Tree

Sometimes our life is no more than the names we give:
Joseph moved us to Missouri,
and the women loved my *Jacob's Tears* —
but they knew it as *The Slave Chain.*
In the Texas flatland winds, *Texas Tears*
lay across the bed, and after the last move
we slept warm beneath *The Road to Kansas.*
That was many droughts and storms ago.
The colors still blaze enough to shame
a Puritan, and not a seam has given way.
Joseph is gone, but even coldest nights
my *Kansas Troubles* brings me through till dawn.

POTTER

the potter's always praying over his kiln

Winters of smearing hot water
on frozen clay in my shed
have deadened the nerves in my fingers.
Spinning earth between my hands
has worn my fingerprints away.

My recurring dream is a common thing:
to finish some work and claim it as my own.
But I wake to the heating or cooling kiln,
cursed by an art beyond my control.
Fire is a fickle and vicious editor.

Will these words explode or melt beneath my hands?
Dear God, I touch my wife in the night
and cannot feel her skin.
I could kill her, throw myself
into some new life, never be traced.

WHITTLER TO HIS LOVER

I began whittling this branch
as the first of a hundred pegs
for a new old-fashioned cabinet.

Something scared me off,
kept me carving
down to this brown bead
I ask you to wear
for what we can and cannot do.

LOST WAX CASTING IN THE SPECIAL SCHOOL

Who is the artist when the work can be shared?
I carve the intricate animal
in wax—elephant, robin—
then watch my students casting amulets
to offer their parents.
Mary, pressing a creature down
into the carton of soft plaster,
is astonished by disappearance.
With Susan next afternoon
there is no telling her greatest pleasure:
jack-in-the-box flame
popped from the match,
melted wax pouring from plaster,
or molten metal disappearing in.
I might choose David, squealing
as his hammer shatters the mold
to reveal a shining pelican of gold.
Or Tracy, collecting stony bits of mold
on the dresser by her bed, each night
rearranging their chance and jagged shapes.

EXPLAINING GLASSBLOWING
TO A GLASSBLOWER

Breath makes another world here.
The apprentice carries a gather of glass
on the blowpipe to the gaffer's bench,
then rolls the molten glob
on the cold steel plate of the marver
to form a rubbery skin. The gaffer blows the piece.
His helper presses the hot metal rod
(the ponty) against the glass,
the gaffer scissors the glass from the pipe.
Heatings at the Glory Hole allow the detail-work;
cooling in the lehr saves the finished piece.

Art is sometimes defined as magic,
magic as the strange, and the strange
as no more than a sound. Finding the right man,
we could say "sponge," "bucket," "scrub"—
and his skin would prickle
at the world he had found.
We could laugh him off and go on cleaning,
but know less than this man who saw
the new and luminous in our work.

SCRIMSHAW

There are some that make their mark
out on the water with a long stroke,
harpoon heaved from behind the shoulder,
twisting through the blubber.
I hold back, wait for bone.

I look hard around, then knife it all—
even the rigging—in close black lines
on the tooth between my knees.
A man who's lost his foot
deserves to stay away
from flying ropes and trying oil,
but this work's more than fair—
No whale's ever stayed on his own bones,
nor kept a ship beside him.

Watch the flames dance like flukes
in your lamp. No matter how big
the well, how many barrels you bought,
you go dry. And I pitch there on the mantel,
dark lines in the dark, sounding strong.

TRAVELLING WEAVER

They wait with their yarn every day of my life.
The children really do come running
down the ruts to my wagon,
shouting "Weaver! Weaver!"
She waits on the porch, sometimes beautiful,
often not. I talk first of the city,
next of county neighbors she has never seen.
There is food, and coffee.
She goes to the bedroom and comes back
again and again with a year's work in her arms.
The children, long since scattered
by the boredom of our quiet talk,
reappear when I trundle out the loom.
The living room will be mine for the week
as I make her spinning worthwhile: looms are high,
so she cannot dress herself, or the children,
except with my help at summer's end.
Her hands, so busy other days, become still
as she watches me more, the children less.
The cloth seeps out like a rainbow stain.
She says she can see it grow,
and one night she dreams it rises
from the loom and wraps her in a year's warmth.
Like several others she cries the day I finish,
and my leaving thrills the children
down the trail again. I don't look back.
I think, once more, of learning how to spin.

CARPENTER: OF HIS PLEASURES

The second finest thing is handing them the wood
to let them wonder at the smoothness
that makes them feel they could prod
their thumbs into the grain as into flesh.
Eleven sandings to get that sheen
before the varnishing.
                              Taking the twelfth paper,
sanding to remove what I first discern
by touch, then by trusting guess alone—
and after that work, handing it back again,
knowing they'll sense no difference—
that is the finest thing.

STATE CRAFT FAIR: BEREA, KENTUCKY

Between the pines dozens of quilts
flap heavily on lines, out of place
like the wash of some flamboyant hermit.
This is a place to commit suicide—
at every step you are amazed and beaten down
by some excellence.
                              Here is cloth,
fresh as bread from its clattering loom.
Here are stoneware plates
shining with geese you'll never lose to Canada.
And always at your feet,
cut-rate bowls and mugs in crates—
even failure can be beautiful and watertight.

That largest crowd surrounds the Winslow boys.
Henry plays the newest mandolin
while Samuel works beside him on the next,
sanding the frets and laying them on.
Nothing goes wrong. The people stare
as if they had walked into a womb.

OLD MUSICIAN, TUSCALOOSA, 1859

He could have picked clean and true
on stretched threads of cornsilk.
He was the singer you hear
in your head when you know
the right sadness could save your life.

They came in the night
and dragged him to the barn,
axed his fingers on the anvil,
sliced off his tongue.

Five weeks later he climbed
from the bed, lifted a mash jug
between his wrists, walked out
to set it on the porch rail.
Bending forward he puffed, slow and resonant,
the day's first song over the pines.

THE WORLD'S LARGEST POET VISITS
RURAL IDAHO

His 300 pounds on his 6-11 frame
will not fit into the dean's VW
waiting at the bus station. He must wait again
while a 40-mile round trip brings another car.

At the Pine Tree Motel the world's largest poet
piles baggage on the underlength bed,
naps on blankets on the tile floor.

That evening, a low table his only podium,
he ducks and squints to read his poems.

Both he and his hosts are aware of all this.
They have him for the glaciers and wild birds
that spring from his giant fingers.
He's there because the battered humming
in his head will not stop.

NIJINSKY: STEP ONE AND STEP TWO

Doctors sliced open your feet
in search of magic—nothing in the bones
explained the jumps that let you leave the earth
for longer than any man.

You held like an osprey above the stage,
riding something we could not see.
As blandly as others cough or cross the street,
you said
"I merely leap and pause."

TO AN EX-STUDENT, ON LEARNING
SHE IS A WORLD-CLASS GYMNAST

for Ann Woods

What routines you must have mounted
in Mycenae and Greece
while the rest of us studied texts
in our windowless room:
Your chalked palms know
they can vault the Cretan bull's horns,
your spine curling down
to the rough, frothing beam of his back.
In the Test of the Bow, you dance
across the axe-helves, beggaring
even the hero's threaded shot.
You sit with a hand on Homer's thigh
as that night's *Odyssey* becomes itself.
As the poet fights
the strange and familiar magic of his brain,
your touch reminds him
the tongue is first a muscle.
Your silent sprung flights and twistings show
what the body of his song can be.

EX-PILOT IN FLIGHT

This way I am still with my plane.
Between chores, while others gather
in the galley or tidy aimlessly,
I will enter the cabin once more.
Over their shoulders I watch
the dazzle of switches I still know blind,
the computerized rush into darkness,
the pilot's fingers grazing the controls.

Hammer, anvil, stirrup.
They seemed such powerful bones,
nothing to be broken
in a backyard fall. I stay on my feet
to feel the plane's rush when I walk.
There are so few ways to leave the earth.
You see, I can still help—
cushioning your shoulder with a pillow,
handing you this icy cup of milk.

ON BEING NAMED LITERARY EXECUTOR
IN THE EVENT OF YOUR DEATH

for Lola Haskins

Given a stone-filled box
marked "feathers," one's hands would drop
toward the floor, fighting to grip
what seems a jolt of magic.

Arriving with bills and casual notes,
your letter asks me to enter
your poems as guardian, judge, prophet.
I must finish you,
give the world the version it deserves.
Should the blossom be rose or mimosa?
Should the food be smilax or corn?
There can be no mistake. Even nightmare
must be perfected, and blank spaces measured.

No one could hold this box without dying
into it: giving himself to falling,
as if some tired goddess had begged him
to rise and sustain the earth.

BAPTISM FOR THE DEAD

*The Mormon Church urges members
to trace their ancestry back at
least four generations in search
of photographs of relatives who
were never baptized into the faith.
These can then be saved by perform-
ing a baptism for the dead.*

I   THE ANGEL MORONI

*A person's face shall be his soul.
This one invention shall be God's instrument.
These glass plates shall have the weight of stone.*

II   ESTELLA MANWEARING BROCKBANK

I'm on the right, not quite touching mother.
I recall Mr. Anderson first
in Jacob Smith's yard. At our place
he put Jane and Carrie's elbows
on mother's lap, and me to the side.
That's why I looked at the camera
instead of praying. Mother scolded me later.
The picture man said he'd never seen
anything so white as those three gowns.
Two years after the picture, when I was eleven,
a landslide killed my sisters in Colorado.
That was seventy-four years ago.
When Mr. Francis found the negatives
in that Springville basement—thousands—
word spread there'd be many we could save.
Mr. Francis had Salt Lake City
pounding at his door. Three men broke in,
smashed dozens of plates
searching the dark faces for their kin.

Isn't mother's face as bright as her medallion
in the light, there on the right side?
Carrie was four, Jane was six.
I touched their small faces
in the tabernacle, and the elders touched them.
I swear mother's face was brighter afterwards,
and the angel Moroni was in the air.

III THE KEEPER OF THE PLATES

Without the names others bring,
the faces I make are nothing.
I've printed hundreds of folks
still trapped in my studio.
Look at these ten under the trees—
only three have been named.
Sometimes I wish I could send the others back—
white leaves and white grass around them,
black hands in their laps,
white eyes glowing with an unknown chance for grace.

VIRGINIA WOOLF

1882-1941

Everything in your life led here.

The threads you saw connecting
all others with yourself were real,
but did not stop there as you thought.
Those wiry silks bored on through
the hearts of those you knew and cared for,
curved and turned to bring themselves
sinewing to this March and wartime bank.

Waves always charged and whipped your senses,
waves of color, scent, sound, beauty,
waves in folds of a green silk dress.
You were the diamond shore of your world,
all waves roaring into you—
waves of blood, friendship, politics, madness—
then refracted out purified to water,
always running, clear but uncontrolled,
here to the River Ouse.

You were your own glacier.
Through fifty-nine years the bone splinters,
blue petals, oak trees of your life
inched toward this stream's melting power.
Then, as your rock-weighted body
settled in, nature's rules collapsed:
when you reached bottom
your flesh and stones became water, while
the stream became the glacier
and your body would not move
from its ring of glowing ice
in a hundred thousand years.

SELF-DESTRUCTING POEM

Boiling down
is for maple syrup
whale blubber
the cabbage of song

The earth
is not something
buried within a tree
You are not
flesh melting to oil
The pot holding this
black vegetable
must froth and boil
over

EVENING RAIN-WALK LIGHTS SHINE IN MOONLIGHT LIKE THE EYES OF LI PO HERE ABOVE MY DESK

In the shallows, the heron gray against black.
She bursts from stillness
kwawking like a crow,
driving a yard above the water,
sucked into the far darkness.

After rain, in the road by the lake
quartz glitters asphalt
in the streetlight glow
like frost on fields of ash under moon.
Around the lamp insects glide and jerk

like raindrops in a vacuum. Uphill
from the lake, the leaves
dead by the road
cup drops of rain.

THE LAST MAGICIAN

We remember from childhood three magicians:

the one cutting women in half
driving swords through midgets in boxes
making grown elephants disappear;

the one with cards and coins
coming and going,
in at your nose
out from his ear,
growing in number
or changing faces
at a wink
or the rub of a palm;

the one dropped from an ocean pier
manacled, cemented, gagged
as he disappeared, absolutely gone
for ninety seconds, then bobbed back
toward the leaning crowd,
sputtering and free.

The machinery we come to accept,
the gifted muscles we admire
yet sometimes catch in their act.
But this Houdini, taking weights on his pale body,
dropping to perform on a stage
we can barely imagine,
remains.

II   LOVES

LOVE: A DEFINITION

He remembers a room
wind blew across, a room
where books and silence held
and he expected nothing.

He remembers a door
swung open in the house
somewhere far below, and

he recalls that then the pitch
of breeze through his singing window
was ever so slightly raised.

THE LOVERS VISIT THE MUSEUM

A small room is marked "Nature's Ghosts":
the white shapes are like favorite clothes
mistakenly bleached, their familiarity lost
in disquieting blankness.
The red eyes of the fawn show
so strongly that its pale body,
Cheshire, almost disappears.
The albino brown bat is pinned under glass,
wings like peeled and drying human skin.
His arms, fingers, legs and tail
glow orange, his teeth are translucent.
If he were alive, we could watch
the blood flowing through his body.
If we could set him loose in the night
darkness would shine through
as if he were scarcely there.

Our hands press together to stop
whatever has been draining away.
How much of ourselves can we lose
before we surrender,
how much must we lose to know
we are now some other thing?

GIFTS

I begin with pin-pricks
through the eggshell, top and bottom.
Then, I lay my mouth over one hole
and force, slowly,
the insides out from the egg.
The strands of white and yolk
fall into a bowl.
If I am careful, we will soon have
an empty shell
and a bowl of egg—

Now, you may choose:
This bowl's thick and slippery
remains
which I will rub
on your neck and nipples
and between your legs
as I tell how I love you.
Or, this light clean shell—
translucent, delicately lined—
that you can show to your friends
or, someday, your children.

FALLING IN LOVE AT FORTY

for P.L.H.

One needs it more now.
Adolescence has so much else
to keep itself feeling young.

Yukio Mishima,
approaching middle age,
wrote in his diary
"Today I have learned to move
a new abdominal muscle."

Perhaps I must ask
no more nor less than this:
that the backs of my hands
become suddenly strange,
that I may study them
as my palms enclose your face,
that the veins of what was always mine
somehow come back to me again.

SOFTENING THE WORLD BY YOUR BODY

Knead the dough until it is ear lobe consistency.
—pie crust recipe, Deaf Smith
Country Cookbook

I roll each politician between my palms
until he changes from my elbow
to the inside of your wrist: rough, flaking skin
to a cool white untouched by sun.

I bake the borders of every country
until they are the two-inch valley
from the base of your spine
down into the cleft of your buttocks—
a petal-soft mystery whose only secret
is that no beauty can fight against itself.

I touch this warm new earth to my lips
to prove it is the hollow of your neck
just above the clavicle—a planet whose windpipe
and vocal cords are so near the surface,
we need only listen to her breath and the words
she makes, and she might be ours forever.

THE BUTCHER'S DAUGHTER TO HER LOVER

for Janet

Swinging on the meat hooks after school,
father yelling when I kicked the hanging sides.
Barrels of guts and bones in the walkway
between shop and house, cats and flies swarming—
when I'd pass too near the barrels
the cats would follow me to the dusty yard
licking my ankles and the tops of my feet.
Mother did all the work—sawing, slicing,
weighing—while father sat all day
as if he'd just dropped down to rest.

If I let you touch me now, you must promise
not to sink into a chair, never to rise.
You must not fall apart
in scraps of red and white.

THE UGLY STEPSISTERS

We hobble blind through the world—alive.
What would you do to be touched by the prince?
Toss your own toes under the bed
before he entered, sit with your back turned coyly
to slide your bloody foot into the slipper?
What would you give for that ride beside him?
The parading moment with the castle in sight
before those pigeons cried you down:
"Look, the right bride sits at home!"
Even after the thing you loved was given,
once more, to the beautiful, would you limp and crawl
to the church dreaming of one more chance?
When those damned pigeons gouged your eye
but left you with one to watch the wedding,
when you knew they would be waiting after in the trees,
would you leave the church to walk home, knowing
you were right?
                    Beauty loses nothing when it pays court
to ugliness. We cried when we saw how she fixed our hair—
what could we do but ask for more?
In some far corner of the earth, beside her skin
old blood stains the deepest recess of the slipper.
We feel it still, that moment when we made it fit.

MARRIAGE

Would you rot for me if I asked?
Most of it would be easy—like trees
quiet there side by side, almost touching,
tending to look the same year after year.

The surprise would come from the inside,
working outward ring by ring
in a sad race from pith to cortex.

The question would be who cracks first
in what gale, spattering at the break-point
into spongy pieces as shocking
as a house you could squeeze in your fingers.

The final mystery would occur
when one, falling, strikes the other:
could the stronger stand,
witness the explosion against itself?
Or will the falling one drive through
the softening core, Baucis and Philemon
disintegrating like planes in collision?

These are my wedding proposals.

PRAYING MANTISES

You said, Before they even begin she bites off his head.
Then, like some miniature green chicken,
he mounts her. Transformed to pure body,
he thrusts and thrusts for hours.
All the while she is twisted back toward him
gnawing at his trunk, his legs,
whatever she can reach that remains.
At some moment in a six-hour span,
the eaten stump fulfills its task.

There was no way for me to believe this,
as you knew, so you took me to your garden.
It was the right time of the year, you said.
We waited, and soon saw,
like exploding orchids on high-speed film,
the superstition of the "little death"—
saw her
gone mad in her multiplying demands.

We are not like this.
Of course we've known destructive loves, but now
we know enough to keep our metaphors where they belong.
We know the distances between mating and loving,
between poetry and our bodies.

THE FAMOUS WAVING GIRL

Florence Martus, 1843-1908

Forty-four years you stood on the cliff
before your island home, waving
a white handkerchief to every ship
in or out of Savannah's harbor.

Some sailors leered through the spyglass
at a young girl, years later laughed at an old woman.
Most dreamed of your swaying silhouette—
made you the mother in a Bristol graveyard,
the lover on a Portsmouth widow's-walk,
the wife never found on any shore.

You began with a child's gesture:
setting down *Wuthering Heights,* raising an arm
to match your white cloth against the sails.
Young men waved back—the connection made.
Frequent returns to the cliff became
constant vigils at the bedroom window,
became the drawer of kerchiefs washed by hand,
ironed, piled flat for uncreased fluttering.

Early on you dreamed of surrender,
daring your coquettish scarf to fall
upon the passing decks below.
Later came the hope for escape,
the white flag of desperation.
They shouted, they furled and unfurled banners,
their signal-fires reddened the sea's black,
but on they sailed for half a century.

The white handkerchief. At the end,
the last bleached leaf of the island's only tree,
your own bones waving in your hand.

FOUND TITLE:
TERESA'S DOLL WITH BROKEN ARM AND COMB

This small white box in this locked car
displayed for all who pass
close enough to notice
its legend detailed with such care:

The sad child, the lonely parent,
neither willing to let the ruined go,
agreeing to set the thing aside for now
in its own marked place. The quiet
choice of the comb as the token
to cheer the lost friend, the child
knowing already the need
for smoothing snarls every day.

The years pass, the girl and the woman
carry the box from one house to the next,
taping it tighter each time,
wondering if they could open it,
what might get out.
They bring it off the closet shelf at last,
place it on the mantel,
read the message every time they pass,
wonder what has happened inside.

They put the box on the rear-window shelf
and drive the car to this parking lot.
Young woman and old woman, walking away.

IN RANEY'S CAVERN

The young tour guide extends a green-sleeved arm
toward a light switch on the rock face.
As her hand flips the switch she stops talking
for the first time since we lunged
through the turnstiles and down beneath Raney's Mountain.
She lets us feel it alone for ten or twenty seconds:
pressing our faces, loosening our children's fingers,
trying to tip us over the iron rail we clutch.
I cannot tell if I have blinked.
"For most of you this is your first time
in absolute darkness. Left here for several hours,
many of you would go mad." Her programmed voice,
accented, lifted and lowered in all the wrong places,
is suddenly beautiful. Some story of Indians,
smugglers, and Civil War deserters—men who used this dark
to shape a life impossible above.
Her words blur toward music, coming at me
from every side. Even the toddlers are silent.
My sense of balance gone, I could die here
but for the singing of this girl—whose thoughts as she sings
must be with hamburgers, with Friday nights
roaring down Raney's Mountain in her boyfriend's Chevrolet.

THE TAXIDERMY SHOP

His neck turned sharply, the hawk reaches
to preen the bright and perfect feathers.
On his haunches the squirrel
sits and holds the dry kernel.
We make our way past rows of stillness.
There is no animal, no energy,
that skill cannot sculpture in this place—
to cut open, empty, and refill
is the labor of those who are here.
What goes in is solid, different—
what went out lies drying in some pile.
Your breath, the same breath, moves on my neck
as you look past me to the marlin
arched in his leap from a sea of tile.

Outside, I drop your hand, turn
to the beach littered with fishbones,
to the wind wearing my skin away.

MIGRATION

To this small hill in Mexico
comes every Monarch butterfly alive.
You can lie on the grass and be covered
with hundreds of bright and weightless bodies.
From a short distance off, you will appear
as a shimmering black and orange angel
burning against the hillside. You can think
how the rest of the world is empty
now of this beauty which buries you here.
It will leave for fifty weeks,
but will return in different bodies
to this same place, and will light upon you
if you are here. Can you refuse these rests,
these hair-like legs brushing you until it seems
they could lift your skin into the sky?

POLAR BEAR SWIMMING IN SOUTH CAROLINA

I would be finished with beasts,
who overrun our poems
as if men and women had hidden
somewhere in the forest, unable to emerge
till keener senses scout the clearing.
But I am underwater with this bear,
staring through a porthole to his pool
as he rolls like an amoeba on a slide,
his yellow fur the slightest excuse
for containing his fluid moves.
Lolling on his back,
he suddenly noses over and dives.
Forelegs back against his sides, black nose a beak
leading his straight drop, he snags his prey:
a knotted mass of leather, bleached white
by its days in the pool.
Then, a rising bubble, the bear lifts out of sight.

I run upstairs to see what has emerged,
but find only that old lumbering body,
its butt too large, its hanging face
that of a witless man who hides no secrets.
Soon, bunching his feet at the pool's edge,
he tips forward as if he'd lost his balance,
unable to recall the ease that awaits him.

His card says the Carolina sun
suits him as well as Arctic ice,
and this snowless land is where we need him.
The coat that keeps him warm keeps him cool—
any air that surrounds him seems the best.

CONDITION: PACHYDERM

1. ELEPHANT EARLY-MORNING

Waking, I find the elephants
everywhere performing
tasks thought before to be human.

My first vision—
a well-tuskered rogue
in green coveralls
straddling the driver's seat
atop a yellow snowplow—
strikes me just so: a vision.
Short sleep, early winter ground-fog,
music blare as I drive the empty streets—
all things join to explain all things.

2. SHORT-ORDER ELEPHANT

The glare of the 7 a.m. diner
explodes evasions:
behind the counter
a pleasantly wrinkled two-ton cow
stands gracefully with rocky-round feet
resting on the counter-top.
She trumpets to a drowsy human customer,
his head hanging,
staring at his coffee cup
flanked by giant feet.

Through the order window
a young bull can be seen
flashing about the grill.
His trunk curls the spatula
swirling and chopping scrambled eggs,
a snowy chef's hat
balances on his great skull.

Stomach deadened, I burst the doorway
running to my car . . . race off.

3. ELEPHANT GRACE

My car skids down icy streets,
soon plows two-foot drifts of country roads.
Miles from the city, heart slowed,
I brake at a sudden roadside scene:
on a fire-pond beside a rotted barn
two yearling cows skate with awesome grace.
Hind legs flow on blades on heavy ice,
front legs wave with Olympic medal form,
trunks swing in perfect rhythm.

Hands shaking, car clumsy with snow,
again I flee.

4. APOTHEOSIS ELEPHANTINE

Back in the city,
cold noon sun crusting snow,
bladder bursting with fear and fullness,
through back door of same bright diner,
slouch the hallway to the john.
Inside, the chef stands at the left-most urinal.
He turns, great wanger
three feet pendulous, half-foot thick.

He plods two-footed out-of-doors,
I follow entranced.
Swooping his cock between the great stumps of his feet,
he writes this message
on the unbroken snow:

> *consider all possibilities,*
> *presume no conclusions.*

NUDE MAN TOSSES MEAT FROM TRUCK

Shelbyville, Ind. (UPI)—State
police arrested a man they said
stood naked on a moving truck
in sub-freezing weather and tossed
sides of beef onto Interstate 74.

Johnson Watson, you sonofabitch,
chucking beef on the highways of America,
blocking the arteries of capitalism—
what were you up to?
Clothed you could have been cagey or malicious,
naked in icy Indiana you had to be mad.

> "Troopers said Watson, 23, hurled
> the meat from an Aurora Packing
> Co. refrigeration truck and then
> took off his clothing and threw
> it off, too."

Whatever it was thrown for, or toward,
the meat wasn't enough. Your clothes had to follow
the fat-glistening carcasses.
The wonder is, you didn't throw yourself.

> "When the refrigeration truck
> stopped, the meat thrower jumped
> to the ground and took off,"

Johnson Watson, the meat thrower,
terror of the midlands by night:
'Nude man forages smokehouses
of Indiana farms, heaves pork
through kitchen windows....'
'Naked thrower rifles meat cases
of Indiana's all-night supermarkets....'

"Trooper Steve Jennings arrested
Watson, who said he was from
Janesville, Wis., and had thrown
the meat to 'feed the people.'"

Johnson Watson, the Robin Hood of beef!
You envisioned the peasants of America
gathering the venison of the New World,
but they didn't come.
Best thing for you, Johnson.
There would never have been enough.
They would have ripped the meat
and stuffed it in their gastanks
to fuel the cars to chase you with.
They would have force-fed your clothing
to their children. They would have taken
you, raw, from the truck.

"He was charged with public in-
decency and malicious trespass."

Democracy, the great leveller,
scythe of America's uneven fields—
Lear would have been jailed before the heath had calmed,
Columbus chained the moment he set foot
on this free and private soil.

SITTING ON EACH OTHER'S LAPS

to Heather at age 4

Blood oozing from tail-stumps
and down the backs of their legs,
the mice run through the dark farmhouse.

Under the tree, blood from the baby's crushed face
runs across splintered wood.

If you knew what I was doing
you would not let me write this—
this desecration of rhymes I've taught you.
You know these things as facts
without cause, without effect.
You would hold me in your arms
with what singing words you know,
the knife and the falling would drift away,
and soon it would be time to sleep.

MY DAUGHTER'S NIGHT

Bees in the ceiling's corners,
tree-shadows on your fingers and sheet,
you lie awake from evening to dawn.
Your little sister sleeps beside you
while strings of black air push through
the window screen to tangle
with voices from walls
and drop quivering in a dark mass
on the dresser across the room.

Though you are nearly seven, you won't believe
you sleep. How do I explain
what I cannot show you?
What if you are right?
Perhaps while my nights are elsewhere
you know the dark as being here.

Your pillow rushes against your ear
like the ocean shell in your closet.
You lie in thought until the daylight
brings us to you from our waste of sleep.

When you're old, what will matter—
that you were always awake,
or that you could never dream?

TOOTH

This morning you'll buy candy or raisins
while I'm left here with this dead bit of mouth.
I've cut your hair and trimmed your fingernails
but this, this white pebble, is something new.
Seven years ago my sperm changed and gave
forth every part of you in a moment—
now, I have crawled across your room in darkness,
given you your belief in magic
and come back with my skeleton in my hand.
Knife-edged where the root has given way,
its hollow center crusted with your blood,
this tooth first seemed far from your perfect smile.
But laid now on my thigh as I sit,
this calcium seed roots in my groin
and blossoms toward my tongue
bearing the secret of our faces.

TRACKING DEER WITH MY DAUGHTERS

From the porch we watched them bound
across the long lawn and full-tilt,
somehow, through these branches
even a six-year-old must lift aside.

I show you the cleft twin-pointed prints
inch-deep in the pine forest loam.
Where the ground goes hard
along a small ridge, mounds of needles
mark the strikes of running hooves.

You track downhill from the house,
refuse to turn back
until a fence and creek arrowhead before us.

A twig snaps in the thicket
beyond the creek. You set your patience
against the deer's — I, mine against yours.
And nothing happens.

And the buzz of insects blends
with that pressure in the forehead
you do not feel—
that humming of moments
when, knowing nothing else, we know
some gain or loss is taking place.

Tomorrow, the apples on the lawn
will once more draw the quarry into view,
and having learned pursuit
you will lead me out again.

ABOUT THE ARTIST

Coco Gordon, born in Italy in 1938, grew up in New York City and attended art classes as a child at the Museum of Modern Art. She made her first artbook at the age of four, earned a degree in art from Adelphi University, and in 1978 established the Water Mark Press. She is a papermaker, poet, sculptor, engraver, printer, and bookmaker, and she designs performance art that involves simultaneously many of her different interests. For the original 1981 edition of *The Last Magician*, she did the engravings, designed the overall format, and—for the hardcover editions—supplied handmade paper for the covers and dust jackets. She and Water Mark Press are currently located in Manhattan.

photo *Brandon Kershner*

ABOUT THE AUTHOR

Stephen Corey was born in 1948 in Buffalo and grew up in Jamestown, New York. He earned a B.A. (1971) and M.A. (1974) in English at the State University of New York at Binghamton. From 1972-1975 he worked as a reporter for *The Post-Journal* in Jamestown; in 1975 he moved with his family to Gainesville, Florida, where he completed a Ph.D. in English at the University of Florida (1979).

In 1977, he and Edward Wilson founded *The Devil's Millhopper*, a poetry magazine. Corey co-edited that magazine with Wilson (1977-1978) and then with Lola Haskins (1978-1981) before becoming the editor (1981-1983). He left *The Devil's Millhopper* in 1983 to join the staff of *The Georgia Review* at the University of Georgia in Athens, where he is currently the Associate Editor.

Since the initial publication of *The Last Magician* in 1981, Corey's other collections have been two chapbooks, *Fighting Death* (State Street Press, 1983) and *Gentle Iron Lace* (Press of the Night Owl, 1984), and a second full-length book, *Synchronized Swimming* (Swallow's Tale Press, 1985). His poems have appeared individually in many magazines, among them *The American Poetry Review, Poetry, The New Republic,* and *Yellow Silk.* His reviews and critical articles have been published in *The Virginia Quarterly Review, Poet and Critic,* and other journals.

Corey lives in Athens with his wife, Mary, and his two daughters, Heather and Miranda.